THE
WONDER
HORSE

First published 2025 by
FREMANTLE PRESS

Fremantle Press Inc. trading as Fremantle Press
PO Box 158, North Fremantle, Western Australia, 6159
fremantlepress.com.au

Designed by Dani Lurie, Balloon Dog Studio, balloondog.studio
Printed by Everbest Printing Investment Limited, China

A catalogue record for this book is available from the National Library of Australia

ISBN 9781760995034 (paperback)
ISBN 9781760995041 (ebook)

Department of
Local Government, Sport and Cultural Industries

Fremantle Press is supported by the State Government through the Department of Local Government, Sport and Cultural Industries.

Fremantle Press respectfully acknowledges the Whadjuk people of the Noongar nation as the Traditional Owners and Custodians of the land where we work in Walyalup.

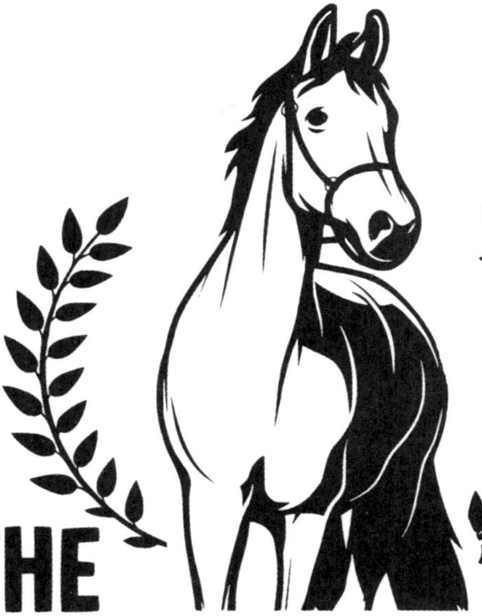

THE WONDER HORSE

MARK GREENWOOD

HISTORY HUNTER

For Mum

INTRODUCTION

Do heroes shape history? Or do tough times create them? In the search for an answer, we delve into the past to explore the stories that inspire us. Evidence found in books, photos and films takes us back to a time when hope and courage played a vital role in defining our national spirit.

In 1929, the US stock market crashed, sending countries worldwide into the Great Depression. The crippling financial catastrophe caused massive social disruption. Unemployment skyrocketed. Hungry people queued for food. In dark times, a hero was needed to lift the spirits of ordinary Australians. The call was answered by an underdog with unflinching courage who refused to be defeated when the rules were stacked against him.

The story of the Wonder Horse involves a web of mysteries, from the intuition of a struggling horse trainer to the baffling puzzle of genetics that transformed an unwanted animal into a champion. At the story's heart is a bond of trust forged between a young man and a magnificent animal.

Ultimately, the greatest mystery revolves around what happened to the people's champion when he was at the peak of his powers. After defeating all rivals in Australia, the beloved horse sailed to the United States to compete in the richest horserace in the world. What occurred there would secure his legendary status and spark one of our nation's most enduring mysteries.

Join me as I delve into the story of the Wonder Horse — Phar Lap.

THE END

At the height of his fame, Phar Lap was enjoying a well-earned rest at a luxurious forty-four-acre ranch in San Francisco. After defeating America's champion thoroughbreds, decisions were being made about his future. Phar Lap's owner, David Davis, was in California sifting through lucrative offers to compete in an ambitious American racing schedule. Movie deals were being negotiated with Hollywood producers for the 'Wonder from Down Under' to star in a series of blockbuster films.

Each day, between 3 pm and 4.30 pm, thousands of admirers visited the Menlo Park ranch to meet 'Big Red' — one of many affectionate nicknames bestowed on the gentle giant. Under the watchful eye of Tommy Woodcock, Phar Lap's inseparable companion, fans lined up to take photos and get close enough to pat the

Phar Lap and Tommy, 1932.

Museums Victoria. Ref. MM 106658.

horse regarded by many as the greatest in the world.

After the crowds left, guards kept watch outside the stable. At all times, precautions were taken to keep Phar Lap safe. He only ate feed imported from New Zealand. He never drank water unless Tommy tasted it first, and he only ate sugar cubes from Tommy's pocket. Every night, Phar Lap's trusted companion slept in a bunk opposite the horse's stall, while the vet and other members of the Australian entourage partied until late, soaking up the celebrity of their association with the champion racehorse.

On 5 April 1932, Tommy woke before dawn to greet his best mate. That morning, Phar Lap refused his usual lump of sugar. Tommy touched the horse's nose. It was hot. He felt under the blanket. Phar Lap was sweaty and running a temperature. Tommy roused the vet, Bill Nielsen. 'Come quick,' he said. 'Something's wrong.'

A common stomach and intestinal disturbance was initially diagnosed. The vet concocted a medicinal tonic, forcing the large capsule down the horse's throat. 'Keep him on his feet,' he told Tommy, 'until the medicine takes effect.'

But the horse showed no signs of improving. His temperature increased. He began retching and displaying signs of distress. He appeared to be in extreme pain and it was becoming progressively worse. Phar Lap pawed the ground with his forefeet. Within hours, he was staggering, barely able to stand.

Bill Nielsen left the ranch to fetch another vet for a second opinion, leaving Tommy alone with a desperately ill horse. Tommy felt helpless as Phar Lap squealed and groaned. His mate was in a dreadful state. Tommy walked the horse back into the stables to make him comfortable. Phar Lap nosed Tommy affectionately under his arm, then he collapsed at Tommy's feet, his head bumping the side of the stable door. It was as if something inside him had burst.

Tommy cradled his beloved horse, sobbing as he stroked Phar Lap's head and mane.

LOT 41

Four years earlier, on a hot afternoon in New Zealand, the last horse in the yearling auction was offered for sale. Lot No. 41 was a lanky fifteen-month-old, foaled in a picturesque paddock in Timaru.

Entering the sale ring, the clumsy chestnut horse with a small white star on his forehead tripped over his long legs. He lacked the poise of the thoroughbreds that had graced the ring earlier that day. Lot 41 wasn't rated highly.

Even a bargain price was unaffordable for a struggling Australian trainer — but Harry Telford had a hunch. Year after year, he'd wasted money on inexpensive horses, hoping to train one that would win a few races and pay the rent. None had turned out any good. Harry was broke, but he never gave up on his dream. He sat up, night after night, in rented

Lot 41 at the Trentham saleyards in New Zealand, 1928.

Painting by Barbara Lewis.

Sydney stables, re-reading the crumpled New Zealand sales catalogue. He pencilled a note next to a horse whose breeding he fancied. *There is something special about Lot 41*, he thought.

Intuition or 'gut feeling' is one of life's great mysteries. But is this remarkable phenomenon real? Is it possible that an inner voice guides us? Or was Harry's hunch really informed knowledge? His obsession with Lot 41 was based on the mystery of genetics and a careful study the horse's pedigree chart. Its father (sire), Night Raid, carried the blood of great British stallions and was the great-grandson of the famous Carbine, who'd won the 1890 Melbourne Cup. Entreaty, its New Zealand–bred mother (dam), was a quality black mare descended from a fine pedigree. Although the parents were well-bred, both were underachievers. Their offspring, the ungainly chestnut colt, stumbled as he walked. Harry scrutinised its bloodlines. The further back he went, the more his faith in the animal's potential grew. *This is a perfectly bred horse*, he thought.

Without the money to pay for Lot 41, Harry badgered several trusted horse owners to bankroll the purchase. No one was willing to risk their money on a hunch. Finally, Harry convinced a wealthy American-born businessman, David Davis, to put up the money for the unnamed horse. Harry wrote to his brother in New Zealand with instructions: 'Make a bid for Lot 41 if you can get him under 200 guineas.'

The sweaty stench of horses mingled with dust that hot afternoon in January 1928. At 5 pm, the last horse was led into the sale ring. 'What am I bid for Lot 41?' the auctioneer asked. 'Am I bid 100 guineas?'

Harry's brother raised his hand.

The only other bidder counteroffered at 150 guineas.

'Do I hear 160?'

Harry's brother nodded.

The other bidder remained silent.

'All done?' asked the auctioneer. The hammer fell, and the clumsy colt was sold for a bargain price.

One month later, the nervous young horse arrived

in Sydney, Australia, after a rough trip across the Tasman Sea. David Davis, the new owner, was furious when he laid eyes on the creature. It was skinny, with warts and pimples all over its head. 'You call that thing a horse?' he said. 'I don't want it — and I'm not wasting another penny to train it.'

Harry didn't have the money to purchase the horse himself. He solved the impasse by offering to rent him for three years. 'I'll train and feed him,' he said, 'and enter him in a few races.'

'Alright, Harry,' David Davis said. 'I'll lease him to you, and if he ever wins a race, I'll take a third of the prize money.' A handshake sealed the 'gentlemen's agreement'.

Jockeys and stable hands laughed when they saw the long-legged creature in Harry's care. 'Looks like a cross between a kangaroo and a giraffe,' they joked. Harry ignored their jokes. He was a shrewd judge of horses with high hopes for the awkward young colt with no name.

Aubrey Ping, a medical student interested in languages, often took a break from university studies to watch Harry train his new horse in Centennial Park. He suggested naming the horse Far Lap, an anglicised version of a Thai phrase, roughly translated as 'light in the sky' or 'lightning'. Harry liked the name — but he was superstitious. 'Melbourne Cup winners should have a two-word name,' he said, 'with seven letters.'

'No problem,' replied Mr Ping. 'Replace the F with PH.' And so, the horse was christened Phar Lap.

THE BOY WHO LOVED HORSES

Destiny is one of life's great mysteries, and Tommy Woodcock was destined for a life with horses. His father, a Cobb & Co coach driver, passed on a love of horses to his son. Tommy displayed a natural rapport with them from a young age — the boy loved horses, and they loved him.

By the time Tommy was six, he was riding ponies in high country. He was a quiet boy who preferred the stables to the classroom. After a long day, Tommy was content to sleep on a bed of hay, head pillowed on a saddle.

Old horsemen taught Tommy how to handle horses. They showed him how to clean a horse correctly and position a saddle. He picked up a lot from the old-timers, and learnt that the most important thing was to look after a horse's legs and hooves.

Tommy was twelve when he decided to try his luck in the city, offering his services as a strapper: exercising, grooming and saddling horses. His mother accompanied him on the train to Sydney and stayed with Tommy until he landed a job. His working day began at 4 am, mucking out the stables, brushing the horses, picking stones out of their hooves and raking up manure. At the end of the day, he cleaned the stalls and topped up water buckets. When it came to horses, nothing was too much trouble for Tommy.

As the years rolled by, the simple country lad became a young man with a gift for horses. He didn't drink, smoke or gamble, and he never had much time for socialising. Tommy wasn't shy with people, but he preferred the company of horses, and horses responded to his gentle, caring nature. One of the trainers Tommy worked for was Harry Telford. Tommy was at the Sydney dock the morning Harry collected a horse that had recently arrived from New Zealand. The new owner, Mr Davis, was angry when it came off the boat — he didn't like the look of the poor thing. But Tommy took an instant shine to the cheeky horse after it nibbled his shirt and jacket, then went for his hat. *There is something special about this horse*, he thought. Tommy reached into his pocket and gave the chestnut colt a lump of sugar.

Harry believed the young horse would benefit from gruelling workouts in the nearby coastal sandhills to 'toughen him up'. Each day, after they returned from training, Tommy would find the horse fretting in the stables, sweaty and exhausted. He'd unclip the horse and keep him company while he rested.

Harry was tough on Phar Lap. Tommy was kind, and the horse responded with tender nuzzles. 'Gee, you got a good one here,' Tommy chirped. 'He'll be a champ one day.' In the stables, it was common practice to identify a horse by a 'barn' name. Tommy nicknamed his new mate 'Bobby'.

Harry trained the horse, but Tommy was always Phar Lap's preferred companion. When the horse saw his friend, he came galloping, tossing his head, stamping with excitement. Tommy walked with him, talked to him, ate with him and slept in the stables with him. Phar Lap loved the attention and followed Tommy like a shadow.

The mysterious bond that developed defied explanation, and Harry couldn't help but notice Tommy's special connection with Phar Lap. The young strapper and the horse were content, standing side by side in comfortable silence. *Phar Lap gets frantic if Tommy's out of sight*, Harry noticed.

After workouts in the sandhills and trackwork to strengthen his legs, Phar Lap responded to Tommy's gentle touch — a scratch behind the ears, the tender grooming of his rich chestnut coat. 'All he wants is food,' Tommy said, laughing. 'And plenty of it.'

Within a few months, Phar Lap began to transform into a strong animal with a distinctive air of class. But if Harry was hoping the horse might turn his fortunes around, he was soon to be disappointed. In his racing debut, Phar Lap had difficulty coordinating his long legs. He ran with awkward strides at the back of the

Tommy exercising Phar Lap.

Alexander Turnbull Library, New Zealand. Ref. 1/2-088739-G.

pack. In his first few races, Phar Lap seemed content to lope along at a comfortable pace.

'Be patient' was Tommy's advice. He rigged a hammock beside Phar Lap's stall and tended to his every need, spoiling his 'Bobby Boy' with apples and sugar treats. With extra training, Phar Lap grew bigger and stronger and showed glimpses of potential, improving his finishing position in each race.

Harry Telford owed money to many people when Phar Lap's loping stride secured his first victory. That win transformed the life of the battling trainer. Harry used the cash to repay his debts. While Phar Lap enjoyed a winter rest, Tommy took work with other trainers. But the young strapper had won the horse's heart. Their bond had grown so strong that Phar Lap refused to eat unless Tommy was in sight. 'Come back and work with me and Phar Lap,' Harry pleaded. 'The horse won't take food from anyone else.'

With his trusted companion back in the manger, Phar Lap was content. After training, Tommy always had an uncanny sense of when his friend was uncomfortable. If Phar Lap paced back and forth, Tommy would massage the horse's muscular legs. 'That helps to settle him down,' Tommy told Harry.

Harry and Tommy knew that Phar Lap needed an excellent jockey to get the best out of him. Some riders whipped horses. 'He needs a gentle jockey,' Tommy suggested. 'Someone who doesn't belt him.' Harry set his sights on 'Gentle Jim' Pike, one of Australia's top jockeys.

With Tommy's tender care and Jim Pike in the saddle, Phar Lap ran in three big races and won them all. In the spring of 1929, he rose through the ranks to compete against top-class horses. Travelling by train from Sydney to Melbourne, Phar Lap outclassed the nation's best thoroughbreds. David Davis was happy to share the prize money. The horse he hadn't wanted was breaking race records, winning admirers ... and making enemies.

THE UNDERWORLD

Phar Lap's star was on the rise when the stock market crashed in October 1929. The financial crisis sent the world and Australia into the Great Depression. In times of unimaginable hardship, people looked to national heroes to lift their spirits. Aviator Charles Kingsford Smith had reached lofty standards of admiration after he and Charles Ulm had become the first pilots to fly across the Pacific Ocean. Cricket's batting wizard, Don Bradman, kept smashing record scores to help Australia regain the Ashes in England.

But times were tough, and amid the economic uncertainty, some fathers were forced to leave their families to find work. Other people turned to gambling. They studied form guides and scraped up a few pennies to place a bet on the races. In dark times, Phar Lap was a ray of sunshine. People funnelled their hopes into a big red horse with power and potential.

Horseracing can make and lose vast sums of money for people from all walks of life, whether trainers, high-rolling gamblers, horseracing syndicates or working-class punters. When Phar Lap won his first race, Harry made a lot of money. But gambling attracts trouble, and the industry at the time was populated by unscrupulous gangsters.

The basic bet on a horse is for a win or a place — second or third. Bookmakers make profits by offering different odds on the horses in a race, based on whether they are strong prospects or moderate chances. 'Bookies' even offer tempting odds on horses with little chance of winning.

Once Phar Lap started winning consistently, the racing establishment forced him to carry extra weight as part of its 'handicapping' system. The strategy of handicapping horses with a weight penalty was designed to give other horses a chance to win. But Phar Lap continued to dominate races, regardless of how much the authorities tried to penalise him.

‘He is a gentle horse,’ Tommy told Harry. ‘He doesn’t enjoy being shunted by train to races in Sydney and Melbourne, in carriages that bump around and squeal into stations.’ Phar Lap was happiest grazing on grass in the company of the man he loved. Tommy walked Phar Lap every day to keep the horse fit. He didn’t like training that involved endless circles around the track, and preferred morning walks on the streets when it was foggy and quiet.

In those days, there weren’t many cars. Tommy would lead his best mate for miles, stopping now and then to pick him a handful of fresh, dewy grass. ‘I guess you could say I am a bit soft on Bobby,’ Tommy admitted. ‘He is the best company in the world. I’d do anything for him.’

As Phar Lap’s domination of Australian racing continued, the bookmakers were taking a ‘belting’. The big red horse was unbeatable. His picture hung on the walls of many homes. He captured the public’s imagination like no other horse had done. Everything he did was front-page news, from rolling around in the sand to carrying giggling children on his back to going for foggy walks with Tommy.

'Gentle Jim' Pike enjoyed every ride as Phar Lap outclassed rivals and smashed track records. Race after race, he put on the greatest continuous display of speed and stamina ever witnessed. He left other champions in his wake despite weight handicaps that no horse his age had ever carried.

But not everybody was happy with a horse that always won. Bookies grumbled. Gangsters were losing money. 'Something's got to be done about that horse,' they whispered. Harry was offered money to 'scratch' (remove) Phar Lap from certain races. Tommy was presented with a bribe to 'fix' the horse so he couldn't win. But the lure of riches didn't tempt either of them. 'Off the premises,' Harry ordered the sleazy criminals. 'And don't come back.'

Bribes didn't tempt jockey Jim Pike either. 'All I want to do,' he told the gangsters, 'is to win the Melbourne Cup riding Phar Lap.' When bribes failed, criminals resorted to other tactics. Harry and Tommy received letters and phone calls threatening to injure the horse. 'He'll be shot down like a dingo or run over,' they were warned. 'It could happen today or tomorrow.' There were rumours that Phar Lap would have poison darts shot at him or acid thrown in his eyes.

By the spring of 1930, the stage was set for the most anticipated racing carnival ever. After a well-earned rest, Phar Lap had developed into a magnificent animal. When he galloped, his muscled haunches provided extraordinary propulsion. Sometimes, he appeared to be flying above the turf. 'Phar Lap has the willpower and the determination to win,' Tommy would always say. 'And he's got a big heart.'

The public's idol was in tip-top condition for the next phase of his glittering career. But Phar Lap would have to overcome threats to his life to win a sequence of four of the most famous horseraces in the world, including the Melbourne Cup. His extraordinary form made him a target. Some criminals would stop at nothing to keep him from winning.

Phar Lap racing with jockey Jim Pike, Flemington, 1930.

Charles Daniel Pratt; State Library of Victoria.

The day of the first race of the spring carnival started typically. Before dawn, Tommy led Phar Lap from his stable to the training track, where he removed the waterproof rug and the hood that protected the horse's eyes from the threat of acid. After a gallop before sunrise, Phar Lap was taken back along the side streets to the stables.

Riding a little grey pony, Tommy trotted alongside the champion. His attention was drawn to a parked car that seemed suspicious. Cars were rare near a racetrack at 5.20 am and the registration plate number was handwritten. A newspaper hid the driver's face. The figure in the back seat had the lower portion of his face masked by a handkerchief. Tommy dug his heels into the pony and picked up the pace.

After hearing the engine start and the screech of tyres, Tommy trotted both horses around a corner. Switching Phar Lap to the footpath side of the road, he placed himself and the pony between the approaching vehicle and the horse. The car swerved around the corner and slowed. As it drew level, a shotgun appeared from the back window. Phar Lap reared up and jumped forward as the shot rang out. Tommy was thrown from the pony.

After the would-be assassins sped away, a passing milkman helped Tommy to his feet. Tommy checked Phar Lap for blood, brushing his hands over his legs, hindquarters, neck and face. Miraculously, Phar Lap had escaped injury. Within minutes, a crowd gathered. Everyone recognised the famous horse. 'Is he okay?' they asked.

Detectives rushed to the scene. News of the attempt on Phar Lap's life was broadcast on the radio. The public were outraged. 'Why would anyone want to hurt such a gentle animal?' Tommy asked. A reward was offered, leading to the capture of the bandits. 'I got a good look at the one in the back seat when his handkerchief dropped,' Tommy told police. 'I could pick him out if I saw him again.'

A few hours later, an excited crowd cheered when Phar Lap arrived at the racetrack surrounded by police. They guarded him all the way to the starting barrier, and after he romped to victory, uniformed officers escorted the Wonder Horse back to the stables.

After the attempt on the champion's life, Harry was taking no chances. 'He'll win the Melbourne Cup,' he told reporters, 'if we can get him to the track uninjured.' Secret arrangements were devised to keep the horse safe.

THE WONDER HORSE

While the people of Melbourne slept, Tommy tiptoed around Phar Lap's stable, spreading hessian bags and straw on the ground to muffle the clip-clop of hooves. Harry stood in the shadows as his horse was led out of the stables into the eerie morning gloom.

At 2.30 am, the float carrying its precious cargo sped through quiet city streets. The destination was an 800-acre property with an old disused racetrack eighty kilometres away. Tommy rode in the float. Lumps of sugar helped settle Phar Lap on the moonlit trip. By 4 am, the big red horse was settled into his new surroundings.

The following day, as the champion grazed in private paddocks, rumours began circulating that Phar Lap was missing, presumed kidnapped, perhaps poisoned. The gossip grew more outrageous with each passing hour. Meanwhile, Phar Lap's actual whereabouts remained a well-kept secret. By day, the horse had no visitors. When night fell, a watchman patrolled the property.

Thunderstorms greeted the first Tuesday in November — Melbourne Cup day. Phar Lap enjoyed a sprint around the muddy racecourse. By midmorning, he was rugged and ready for the trip to Melbourne. But heavy rain had flooded the engine of the car that towed the float. Everyone took a turn with the crank. The engine couldn't be started. The clock ticked down. With only two hours until the start of the big race, the motor finally spluttered into action.

Escorted by police motorcycles and a patrol car, the champion finally arrived at the racetrack. Seventy-two thousand people were waiting hopefully to witness their hero win Australia's most prestigious horserace. Phar Lap entered the arena to enormous cheers. Admirers jostled to get a closer look. Tommy scanned the crowd for suspicious-looking characters while jockey Jim Pike waited nervously in the mounting

Phar Lap arrives at the racetrack under police escort.

News Ltd. Newspix NP 1421852.

yard wearing his familiar red jacket, black-and-white hooped sleeves and red cap.

Despite an attempted assassination, Phar Lap had easily won the first race of the carnival. Now, he was about to compete in the Melbourne Cup — the most famous horserace in the country. His legend would be assured with a win.

The starter wasted no time. Carrying an extra handicap of over sixty-two kilos, Phar Lap exploded from the barrier. Jim Pike crouched on his shoulders, clenching the reins, face buried in the flowing mane. At the home turn, Phar Lap clicked into gear with huge raking strides. 'Here he comes,' roared the crowd as their hero hit the front. They erupted in joyous celebrations when Phar Lap cruised past the winning post.

Seldom has a horse received such a reception. 'He's the best horse Australia has ever seen,' Jim Pike said. 'The only chance of beating him is if they breed horses with wings.' No one was more relieved than Tommy. Later that night, alone in the stable, he stroked Bobby's head and gave him an extra lump of sugar.

Two days later, following up on his Melbourne Cup triumph, Phar Lap won the next two races of the carnival, thrashing top sprinters with dazzling bursts of speed. Eight days. Four races. Four wins. Phar Lap was invincible. Newspaper headlines declared him to be the greatest racehorse of all time. Harry Telford and David Davis were raking in more prize money than they could imagine. Harry settled into Braeside, a 143-acre horse training centre in Victoria and a magnificent home for his family.

And Phar Lap kept on winning. He was so supreme that race officials kept tinkering with the rules to end his domination. He was allocated the most severe weight penalties. After one race, Tommy noticed that Phar Lap looked tired. 'He snapped at me,' Tommy told Harry, 'as if to say, "You should know better".' When loaded onto the float, he was trembling. Tommy drew Harry's attention to Phar Lap's swollen leg. 'He's done everything we've asked of him,' Tommy said. 'He's too sick to race for a while. He needs a rest.'

The following year, Phar Lap's weight penalty gave him virtually no hope of winning the 1931 Melbourne Cup. Tommy feared the extra kilos might damage him forever. He pleaded with Jim Pike to take care of the horse. 'Don't worry,' the jockey replied. 'I won't knock him around.'

By now, Harry's original lease on Phar Lap had expired. He purchased a half-share and became an equal owner with David Davis. But both owners were disappointed on Melbourne Cup Day. Harry argued hard trackwork was the way to get the horse back into form. Tommy insisted on light training, but his opinion was ignored. Phar Lap became irritable, a far cry from his usual docile self. He reeled off another string of victories but was now carrying weights designed to end his career. Rumours began to spread that Phar Lap had run his last race in Australia.

Soon, Phar Lap's destiny was confirmed. 'I've accepted an invitation to compete overseas for the world's richest prize in horseracing,' David Davis told reporters.

Harry Telford and David Davis did not see eye to eye on the risks involved in transporting Phar Lap across the open ocean, from summer in Australia to winter in another hemisphere, with the expectation that he could then beat the best horses, but David Davis insisted.

Phar Lap's fame had brought Harry a stable of twenty horses that needed training. Importantly, he had family responsibilities with a seriously ill infant daughter. Harry was committed to staying home in Australia. 'You're the only person I trust,' he told Tommy. 'I want you to go as his trainer.' With Jim Pike unable to keep his weight down to continue as jockey, Billy Elliot, who had previously ridden Phar Lap six times for six wins, would ride the horse in Mexico.

THE ARK

At the Sydney dock, a large crowd gathered to get a last glimpse of their hero. 'Good luck, Phar Lap,' fans called out. 'We're proud of you.'

The first stage of the long journey would include a five-week stopover in New Zealand. Phar Lap's only experience at sea was when he had sailed to Australia as a skinny young horse four years ago. Now, he was leaving as a champion. With Tommy by his side, the big red horse was hoisted aboard the SS *Ulimaroa*.

On board, Phar Lap travelled in the company of a troupe of circus animals. The mighty racehorse's nearest companion was a heehaw donkey who took an instant liking to the straw bedding Tommy laid out. Phar Lap struck up a great friendship with his long-eared neighbour.

It was a rough trip for Tommy, who was seasick

Phar Lap being manoeuvred aboard a ship to the United States, 1932.

National Library of Australia Ref. PIC/15611/6814

for the first two days. 'The horse is a better sailor than me,' he joked. After five days, the ship berthed at Wellington, where thousands of wellwishers met Phar Lap. Harry Telford's brother, Hugh, was proud to welcome the big chestnut horse home to the land of his birth. The travelling Australian entourage was invited to stay at his property at Trentham. Before they left the wharf, Tommy led the superstar around so the crowd could celebrate his triumphant return.

Phar Lap enjoyed the lush paddocks of ryegrass and clover. On weekends, after regular exercise at the racetrack, men, women and children flocked from far and wide to see the champion. Phar Lap was a gentle giant who was especially fond of children. He posed for photographs, and after a few weeks making new friends, it was time to board the SS *Monowai*, bound for the United States.

Tommy made sure everything was ready for the long journey. A large consignment of oats, chaff and hay was loaded aboard. A comfortable stable was constructed on the upper deck to protect the horse from sea spray on rough days and to provide space to enjoy the fresh air when the weather was fine. Thick padding guarded Phar Lap from knocking himself. In a separate area, twelve tons of sand were loaded aboard for a pit for the horse to roll in. Tommy made sure Phar Lap got his daily exercise by parading him back and forth from his enclosure, turning around and walking back to the sandpit.

On the previous trip, from Sydney to New Zealand, Tommy had stayed with Phar Lap. Now they were on an extended voyage, he decided to seek more comfort. But Phar Lap didn't want Tommy out of sight. 'If I was gone, even for a moment,' Tommy said, 'he would make a mighty fuss.' One night, Tommy went to the dining room for his meal. The jockey Billy Elliot rushed in. 'Come quick,' he said. 'The horse is going mad.' Tommy raced upstairs and pacified Phar Lap. When he attempted to return and finish his meal, the horse went through the same performance. From then on, Tommy took his meals where Phar Lap could see him. When Tommy got tired, he would lie down, and Phar Lap would sleep with his big head resting on Tommy's chest.

The weather in the tropics was intensely hot. Phar Lap sweated profusely. Tommy sponged him down three or four times a day to keep the horse cool. The sand roll exercise area was Phar Lap's favourite place. He enjoyed standing on his hind legs, pawing the sea air. Sometimes, he would bail Tommy up in a corner and playfully nip at his sleeves. They talked and played, but after two months at sea, Tommy was pleased that the journey would soon be over.

On 14 January 1932, a day out of San Francisco, Phar Lap neighed and gazed out to sea, ears pricked forward, nostrils wide open. 'He can smell land,' Tommy said. The ship eased into its berth on a cold, grey morning. The precious cargo was winched onto the dock in a wobbly horsebox.

Before Phar Lap regained his land legs, he was besieged by reporters keen to get a photo of the champion, described as the 'Anzac Antelope', 'Red Terror' and 'Wonder from Down Under'. 'I'm in charge now,' Tommy declared. Due to a recent fall of snow, he refused to take Phar's Lap's rugs off for a photo. The photographers' flashlights captured a spirited animal that played up to the crowd at Tommy's expense with a gentle nip on the seat of his pants. 'Be a good boy, Bobby.' Tommy grinned, and the hooded horse followed him into a waiting float.

A long drive took the entourage to the luxurious Menlo Park horse ranch, where no effort was spared to make the Australians comfortable. Tommy let Phar Lap stretch his legs with a long, slow workout. Each day, film stars, business tycoons, politicians and leading racing folk visited the ranch.

The richest horserace in the world, the Agua Caliente Handicap in Mexico, was only four weeks away. After heavy rain, Tommy restricted the horse to light work on the muddy Menlo Park track before they set off on the two-day, 965-kilometre road trip across the US border from California to Tijuana, Mexico.

When the entourage arrived at the Agua Caliente racetrack, Phar Lap stepped out of the float, and the official welcoming party got their first glimpse of his giant frame. Phar Lap was his usual playful self, holding court as the other horses from all parts of the Unites States arrived for the big race.

Tommy chose a barn away from rival horses, who were stabled closer to the racetrack. Phar Lap enjoyed company, so a small grey pony was stalled next door to remind Phar Lap of his little pal back in Australia. A hole was knocked in the wall so they could see each other.

Phar Lap's stable was guarded day and night. Apart from the Australian entourage, nobody went near Phar Lap, and Tommy rarely left the horse's side. To confuse their opponents, training took place in secret before dawn. By the time other horses and trainers arrived, Phar Lap was rugged up, having completed his morning gallops. Rival trainers criticised Tommy's light training methods. 'He's a good horse,' they joked, 'with a silly trainer.'

Everyone thought the 'Wonder from Down Under' would take more time to acclimatise after the long

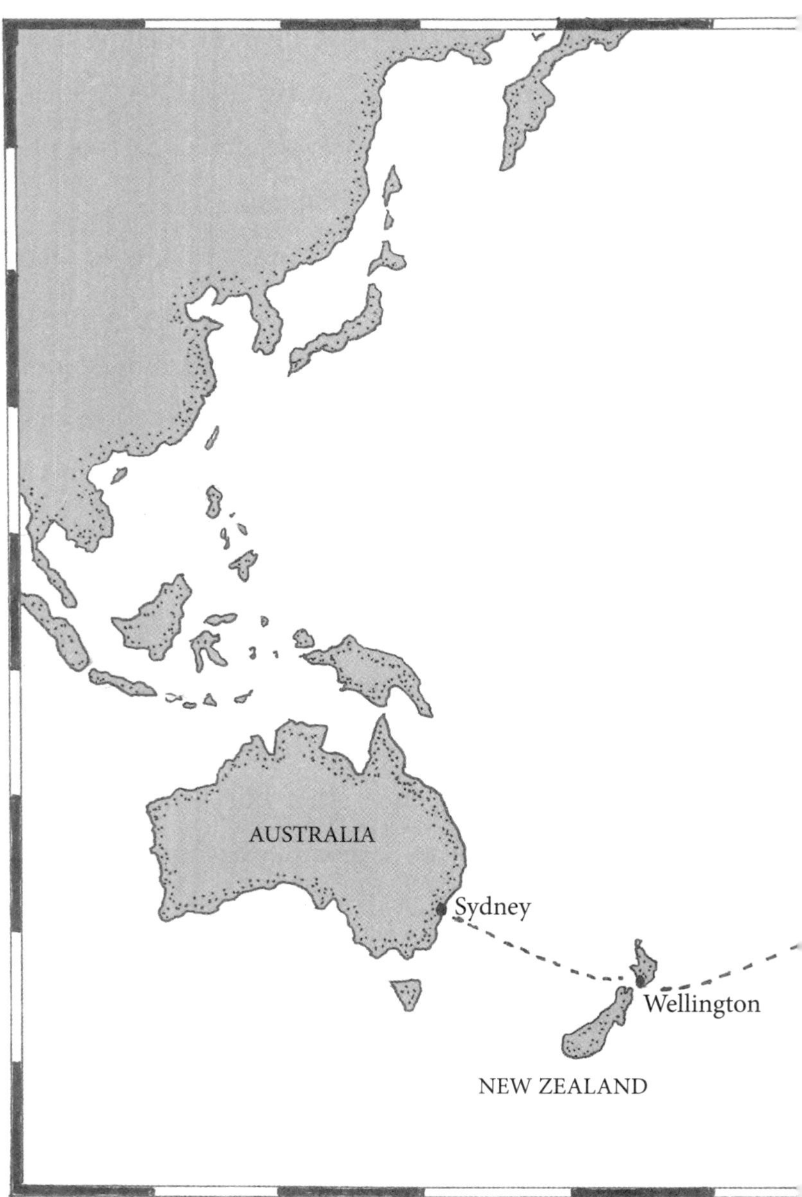
AUSTRALIA
Sydney
Wellington
NEW ZEALAND

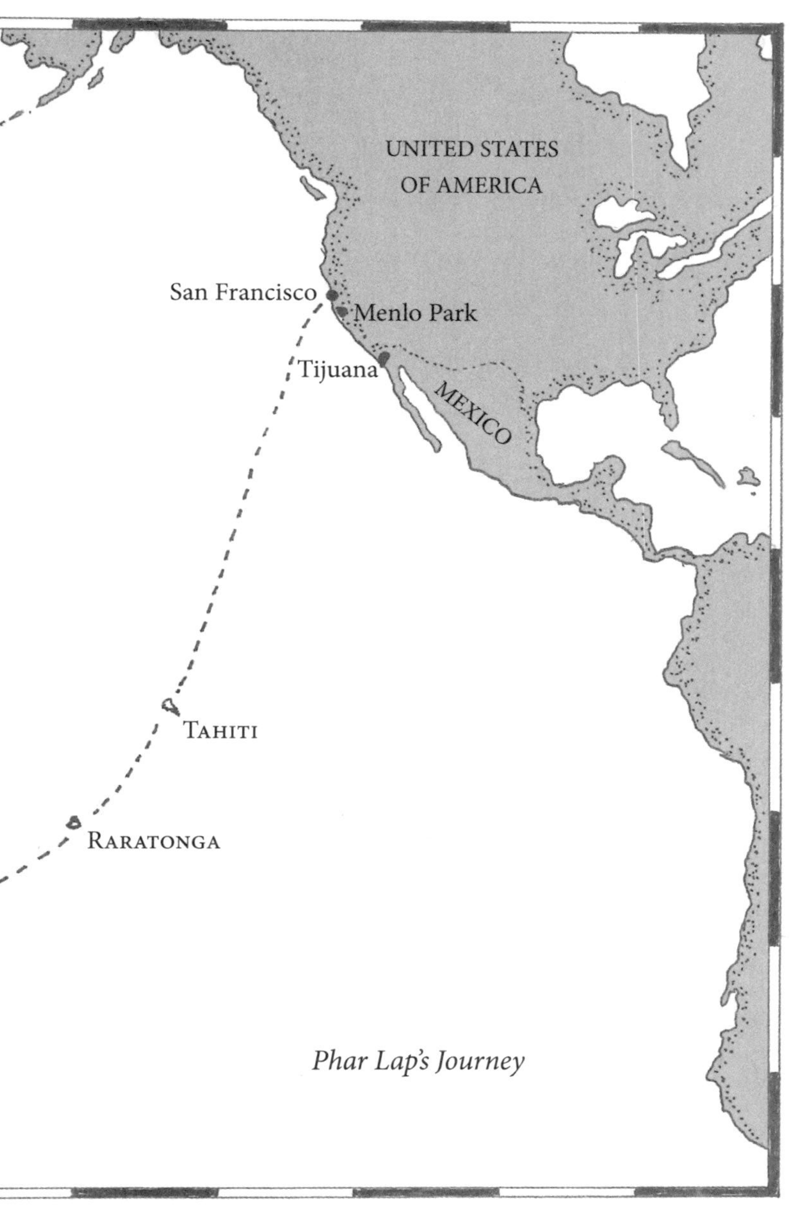

Phar Lap's Journey

journey by sea and then by road. 'He's cherry ripe,' Tommy declared, 'and ready to run the race of his life.'

Then, ten days before the race, disaster struck. A stone lodged in his horseshoe split Phar Lap's hoof. The injury was severe and became infected. *My first time as his trainer, and now his foot is busted*, Tommy worried. Wax wrapping didn't help. A large section of the hoof was loose and hanging off.

Tommy consulted a local horseman. 'What can be done?' he asked.

Jimmy Smith was an expert farrier and had seen such an injury before. 'If he's going to run,' he said, 'you'll have to cut off a large piece of his hoof.'

Under Tommy's supervision, the vet anaesthetised Phar Lap's leg and the risky operation was performed. Recovery began immediately. Tommy painted iodine on the raw wound three times a day. When the pain subsided, Phar Lap was taken for gentle walks on soft sand. Tommy was astonished at the speed at which the hoof responded to daily treatment. While the foot was healing, Jimmy brought in his blacksmith forge and skillfully moulded a set of protective horseshoes.

Three days before the big race, Phar Lap had his first run to test his injured hoof. 'Aw gee,' Tommy said, 'he flew around the track.' Tommy never forgot the look of relief when he informed David Davis that Phar Lap would be a certain starter.

Secretly, Tommy couldn't wait for the race to be over so he could get his beloved horse out of Mexico. Crime flourished there on a scale not known in Australia. Tommy had been warned about gangsters known to 'fix' races, and he'd received an anonymous letter:

> *Be careful. There are unscrupulous men who will stop at nothing to eliminate a dangerous rival. Keep your horse off the rails. Don't let him get hemmed in by the other horses.*

Tommy knew other horses wore sharp blades on their horseshoes to assist with stability in soft dirt. On tight turns, the razor-sharp edges could sever a rival horse's tendons.

THE BADLANDS

A warm breeze drifted in from the desert. It was a perfect day for a horserace. A steady stream of flashy cars crossed the Californian border into Mexico. Trains brought people from Los Angeles and San Francisco. Private planes landed. Hotel rooms were booked out.

The elegant Agua Caliente resort offered an opportunity to cross the border and escape the prohibition on alcohol and gambling in the United States. The casino and hotel and its renowned racetrack attracted gangsters who rubbed shoulders with movie stars and politicians.

Before the race, Phar Lap stood in the holding yard, unfazed by the razzamatazz of the excited crowd. 'You better wake your horse up,' shouted the starter.

'Don't worry,' Tommy said. 'He'll come to life soon enough.'

Jockey Billy Elliot leaned over Phar Lap's shoulder. 'I hope I do the right thing.'

'Don't get caught in a jam with the other horses,' Tommy instructed him. 'Get him on the outside. Give him a clear run. His heart will get him over the line.'

As the main race drew closer, celebrities watching from the grandstand spilled out onto the manicured terraces to catch the action. Upstairs in the gambling parlour, last-minute bets were placed. Eleven top-class American horses took their positions. The Australian horse was up against fierce competition, including sensational gallopers Dr Freeland, Spanish Play and the Kentucky Derby winner, Reveille Boy.

Jockeys were tense, avoiding each other's gaze. A hush came over the crowd. Phar Lap's journey to the starting line had been gruelling, having travelled by sea from Australia to New Zealand and then to San Francisco. From there, he'd travelled by road to Mexico. A severe injury to his hoof had hampered his preparations. Would it hold up to a pounding on a stony Mexican racetrack?

The race exploded with a violent charge. Phar Lap was last out of the gate. The other horses cut across him. He dropped to the back of the field. The first time the pack passed the grandstand, he was eating dust and dirt kicked up by the leading horses. The Australian champion appeared well beaten.

A mile from the finish line, he made up ground. Then, following Tommy's instructions, Billy Elliot took the horse out wide of the pack. Phar Lap rounded the turn, straightened up and made his move. His sudden acceleration caused audible gasps. In the blink of an eye, Phar Lap raced around the outside and went from seventh to hit the front. The Red Terror dazzled the crowd with a withering blast of speed. 'What kind of a superhorse is this?' people asked.

In Australia, the long-distance wireless broadcast occasionally dropped out. Listeners leaned in. 'Come on, Phar Lap,' the commentator's voice crackled down the line. 'Phar Lap, you beauty!'

In Mexico, spectators stood on tiptoes and cheered as the 'Wonder from Down Under' streaked past the finishing post, breaking the previous track record, winning hearts and creating sporting history.

Film stars, gangsters, spectators and race officials — everyone crowded into the winner's circle. Tommy took the horse's reins and led him through the pandemonium. He reached into his pocket for a lump of sugar. 'I knew you could do it, Bobby.' With Tommy by his side, Phar Lap was content as flashbulbs popped, capturing the proud horse from every angle.

But not everybody was happy.

Tommy could hear some angry words behind him. 'They're the toughest looking bunch of desperados I've ever seen,' he whispered to jockey Billy Elliot. When officials tried to drape a garland of roses around the winner's neck, Phar Lap refused the floral tribute and reared up. Backing away, he slipped on a step, injuring the back of his heel. Only Tommy noticed the trickle of blood. The horse nosed his trusted mate, lifting Tommy's arm, a signal to take him away.

Based on that extraordinary victory, highly qualified judges of horses as well as horse owners,

Phar Lap with jockey Billy Elliot and trainer Tommy Woodcock after winning the Agua Caliente Handicap in Mexico, 1932.

Museums Victoria. Ref. MM106656.

breeders, trainers and jockeys rated Phar Lap the greatest racehorse they'd ever seen. The King of England sent a telegram: *Heartiest Congratulations on great victory of Phar Lap — King George V.* Compliments came from the prime ministers of Australia and New Zealand and the Governor-General of Canada.

Late into the evening, Phar Lap's victory was celebrated. One of the world's most famous singers, Al Jolson, entertained the revellers, his voice ringing out to the melody of 'It's a Long Way to Tipperary':

It's a long way to Caliente,
It's a long way to go.
It's a long way across the ocean,
For the richest prize I know …
Goodbye Dr Freeland,
So long, Spanish Play,
It's a long way to Caliente,
And Phar Lap knows the way …

As the festivities continued, the Australians were plotting a quick getaway. The race that sealed his legend had taken a lot out of Phar Lap. He was exhausted, and he'd re-injured his hoof when he reared up to avoid the garland of roses. Tommy was relieved to have the champion rugged up in the float, bound for a well-earned rest at the luxurious Menlo Park ranch back in San Francisco.

THE LAST POST

Sixteen days after winning the richest horserace in the world, Phar Lap woke up displaying signs of distress. Extreme pain became progressively worse. Within hours, he was staggering, barely able to stand, before he collapsed. Tommy cradled Phar Lap in his arms. Tenderly, he stroked his head and mane as the beloved horse took his final breath.

Those who were there that day were numb. Tommy clung to Phar Lap until friends helped him up and escorted him away from the stables. Tommy's heart was broken. The 'light in the sky' was gone. Later, newspaper reporters found him packing away Phar Lap's rug and bridle, tears streaming down his face. His great mate was gone.

Soon, cables were humming, and the news spread around the world.

PHAR LAP SEN

NZAC LEADS REVEILLE BOY TWO LENGTHS

cond Chopped Off Record; Scimitar Third; Victor's Back Stretch Run Amazes

By Chet Koeppel

AGUA CALIENTE, March .—Well the ballyhoo was no eam.

A great race horse, termed e "Terror of the Antipodes," me 10,000 miles from kanga- o land, made his American cing debut with a reputation celed, perhaps, by no thor-

'What a H

PHAR LAP EASY WINNER IN RICH CALIENTE STAK

Reveille Boy Second, Scimi Third; New Record for Course Set

(Continued From First Sport P

ica," they exclai we never saw horseflesh that with him."

Off from the elev tion, Phar Lap wa sixth position at th liott then turned on the half, no one but

PHAR LAP SHOT FIRED

Cup Favourite

(From "Brooklyn.")

MELBOURNE, No which recalls a plot occurred at Caulfie unsuccessful attem the champion race Derby morning a were preparing to see the great hor lea announcer news.

PF

PHAR LAP EN ROUTE TO MEXICAN COURS

Phar Lap

hile Tired Tr ster

ustra

PHAR LAP DEAD.

Attack of Colic from Green Feed.

AUTOPSY PERFORMED.

General Regret for Great Horse's End.

Phar Lap, Australia's wonder racehorse, died of colic on Tuesday fternoon at Mr. Ed. Perry's stock farm at Menlo Park (California).

Rumours that the horse had been poisoned have been strenuously

ATION

PHAR LAP, NOTED RACE

IS DEAD; COLIC

ION HORSE

ENTERITIS

en Collapse

R STAGGERED

BY LOSS

LIGHTNING—PHAR

THE AUSTRALIAN WONDER

What better illustration of the logic of the saying has ever been furnished than what is revealed by the fortuitous ... were associated with the coming into being, and the many episodes — romantic, sensational, humorous, and ... coincidental to the all too short career of the Australian Wonder horse, Phar Lap, whose sudden death from colic, ... Perry's stock farm, at Menlo Park, California, America, on 5th April, 1932.

Phar Lap was Wilfully P

While Tired Trainer Slept, Gangster "Fixed" The Horse

MAN AND WINS MELBOURNE CUP

LAP'S GREATNESS WILL NEVE

BE FORGOTTEN

arisons Wit

C "LAST POST" FOR MIGHTY PHAR LAP SHOCKS NATIO

SPECIAL PHAR LAP EDITION

In Australia and New Zealand, the headlines cast a gloom over both nations. Harry Telford wandered around Phar Lap's old exercise yard. 'You couldn't help but love that horse,' he told reporters. 'Only one like him comes along in a lifetime. Phar Lap was an angel. He could do anything but talk.' Harry leaned on the post-and-rail fence. 'Poor Tommy.' He bowed his head. 'I can't imagine how he's feeling. He loved that horse. They were inseparable.'

The nation's sorrow quickly turned to questions and accusations. What caused Phar Lap's death? Was it an infection — or something more sinister? Everyone wanted an answer.

Initially, the cause of death was suspected to be an intestinal disturbance known as colic. Within hours of Phar Lap's death, the vet Bill Nielsen and the Menlo Park vet, Caesar Masoero, conducted an autopsy. Their report indicated severely inflamed stomach and intestines. Acute infection was, in their opinion, caused by an unidentified 'toxic irritant', as an ordinary case of colic would not have killed the horse in such a short time.

After the autopsy, the mystery deepened when most of Phar Lap's vital organs were rumoured to have been secretly buried in a metal box at an undisclosed location. Despite extensive searches, the metal box has never been found. Days later, scientists at the University of California conducted a second autopsy with the few remaining pieces of intestines and vital organs. Using 'inadequate material submitted for examination', it was concluded that small quantities of poisonous lead arsenate may have caused the inflammation of the intestines, but the factors responsible for Phar Lap's death 'may never be determined'.

Was Phar Lap poisoned? And if so, was the poisoning deliberate or accidental?

Six days before Tommy found the horse in distress, workers sprayed lead arsenate on the west side of the ranch to eliminate caterpillars that had infested the oak trees. Could the spray have contaminated the paddocks? Phar Lap grazed on that grass. In theory, he may have ingested some insecticide, but other horses grazed in the same pastures. None became ill, and the quantities of poison were so small that the insecticide was unlikely to have been the cause of death.

Another speculative theory involves mouldy feed. The Australian entourage was so concerned about someone poisoning their champion that they had brought feed with them. Over time, could old feed have caused the fatal intestinal bacteria? 'All he ate was good tucker,' Tommy insisted. He'd inspected everything Phar Lap had consumed. He wouldn't let the horse drink if he hadn't tasted the water himself. Would a devoted and attentive trainer have permitted his beloved horse to ingest anything that wasn't fresh or may have been harmful?

What happened to the people's champion remains one of our nation's most enduring mysteries. A lingering controversy surrounds Phar Lap's sudden, agonising death. But could one of sport's saddest stories have a 'smoking gun'? Could the evidence that might finally solve the Phar Lap mystery be hiding in plain sight?

SUSPICIOUS MINDS

Everyone wanted an answer. What had caused a healthy thoroughbred at the peak of his powers to die so suddenly? There were so many opinions and rumours. Opposing theories on whether it was poisoning — accidental or deliberate — have remained unresolved since that fateful day in 1932.

Attention turned to Harry Telford's diary, which contained a recipe for a secret 'tonic' that included highly toxic arsenicalis (arsenic). At the time, arsenic was used in horse tonics. But it is deadly poison if given in incorrect doses. Arsenic takes a long time to leave the body, so was a slow build-up in Phar Lap's system fatal?

Another arsenic-based tonic, Fowler's solution, was given to Phar Lap throughout his racing career as

General Tonic

℞

Tinct Nucis Vom. 12oz
Liq Arsenicalis 12oz
Ferri Carb. Sacch 12oz
Syrup Glycerophosphates 2 p
Honey 2 lbs
water to make 1 Gallon.

Give yearlings 2 tablespoonfuls
Two year old 3 " "
3 years & over. 4 " "
over their feed twice daily

This is a great Tonic for all horses

Harry Telford's general tonic for racehorses, with ingredients including Arsenicalis (arsenic).

a ‘pick-me-up’. Horses invariably looked healthy after taking it. On a long voyage by sea, it is reasonable to assume that Phar Lap may have gone off his feed from time to time. Did Tommy supplement his diet with Harry’s tonic, unaware that the horse was building up dangerous levels of arsenic? We know that when Phar Lap arrived in San Francisco, reporters commented that he looked remarkably healthy. But Tommy was never a fan of Harry’s ‘tonic’. In a newspaper interview four years after Phar Lap’s death, he admitted to getting rid of it. ‘At first, I used to argue that a horse like Phar Lap did not need a tonic. Harry would have none of it. So, as time went on, I adopted other tactics,’ Tommy revealed. ‘To please Mr Telford, I would take the bottle and pour a quantity down the drain so he would think I was following his instructions.’

Another theory focused on whether Phar Lap had died of exhaustion and overwork. David Davis admitted that the horse was weakened by travel from Australia to New Zealand. Was the long sea voyage to the United States, followed by an almost

2000-kilometre round trip by truck from California to Mexico and back, too much for an exhausted horse? Did travel, training and a strenuous race leave him vulnerable to illness?

Without a conclusive cause of death, researchers turned their attention back to the original autopsy, which stated that death was caused by an acute infection brought about by a toxic substance that 'could not be identified'. The question remained — was the substance a poison?

In 1932, no one knew of a bacterial infection with a complex name — duodenitis-proximal jejunitis. First recognised in 1977, the disease causes fatalities in seventy percent of horses who contract the infection. Symptoms suffered by Phar Lap are consistent with this bacterial infection that was unknown at the time of his death. It can be brought on by stress, a change of environment, a change of weather, hard racing and travel. Some experts believed all these factors may have caused the inflammation reported in the original autopsies.

An alternative theory is that Phar Lap was deliberately poisoned. Rumours that arsenic tablets were found in the corner of Phar Lap's stall were never proven. If he was murdered, it wasn't the first attempt on his life. In Australia, his life was constantly threatened and he often required police protection.

After Phar Lap's incredible performance in Mexico, it is hard to contemplate that anyone in the United States would dream of murdering the beloved horse. The popular sentiment was that the American sporting public would have paid anything to save Phar Lap's life. Those who saw the last race recognised his freakish talent. Americans love the unusual, and everyone agreed Phar Lap was world-class. After his death, a Los Angeles radio station asked listeners to stand for thirty seconds as a mark of respect. His sudden demise made the front page of *The New York Times*. Importantly, if criminals had wanted to eliminate Phar Lap, it would seem more likely that they would have done it before the race, not after.

Phar Lap's skeleton was donated to New Zealand's

national museum (today known as Museum of New Zealand Te Papa Tongarewa). His handsome chestnut hide, mounted by experts in taxidermy, remains the most popular attraction at the Melbourne Museum. Tommy was moved to tears when he saw it. Today, people of all ages and backgrounds marvel at the exhibition, and all leave with the same question — who or what killed Phar Lap? Could the evidence have been there all along, waiting for modern technology to solve the mystery?

In 2008, scientists Dermot Henry and Dr Ivan Kempson, collected a small sample of mane hair from Phar Lap's mounted hide. Using X-rays generated by a synchrotron, a machine that produces intense beams of light, they were able to peer beneath the surface to detect and map the concentrations and distributions of arsenic in the sample hair cells. The advanced technology allowed them to distinguish between arsenic that had entered the hair cells by ingestion via the bloodstream and arsenic that had contaminated the hair during the taxidermy process. The results of the analysis suggested that Phar Lap had ingested a large, potentially lethal dose of arsenic in the last thirty to forty hours of his life.

Tommy knew in his heart what had happened. Over the years, he pieced together everything that occurred on that fateful day. In an interview close to the end of his life, he said, 'I often wondered if the vet could have mixed up the wrong ingredients. After the horse took the capsule, he kept getting worse.' Is it possible the vet, Bill Nielsen, after initially suspecting colic, gave the horse the wrong medication in the early hours of Phar Lap's initial diagnosis? In the end, Tommy decided to keep some other suspicions to himself. Nothing he could do or say could bring back his best mate.

GONE
BUT NOT FORGOTTEN

There remains a rivalry between New Zealand and Australia regarding which country has the greater claim to Phar Lap. The truth is, the big-hearted horse didn't just win the affection of two nations, he was a hero around the world.

In Australia, the public admires an underdog who succeeds against the odds. In the grim years of the Great Depression, Phar Lap was a hero. In times of great suffering and hardship, he brought joy to people from all walks of life. His sudden death brought two nations to a standstill.

After Phar Lap, Harry Telford failed to train any significant winners. Without further proceeds of Phar Lap's success, he was forced to leave his Braeside home and training facility. He retired from racing in 1957 and died in poverty three years later.

Tommy Woodcock with Reckless
on the night before the Melbourne Cup of 1977.
Bruce Postle; National Library of Australia. Ref. PIC/12321/51.

Jim Pike, the jockey who rode 'Big Red' to many of his great victories, retired several years after Phar Lap's death. Like many jockeys in those days, he often starved himself to keep his weight down. The method of 'wasting' left him with ongoing health problems. He also died in poverty in 1969.

The vet, Bill Nielsen, never spoke publicly about that fateful day in 1932. What happened to Phar Lap's remains that were removed for the autopsy and what was buried in a metal box at a rumoured secret location remains a mystery.

Tommy Woodcock, Phar Lap's beloved companion, won a place in the nation's heart alongside his inseparable friend. Tommy's destiny was intertwined with the chestnut horse from the time it first nibbled his jacket and hat. After Phar Lap's death, Tommy was heartbroken. The memory of that dreadful day at Menlo Park haunted him. He turned down most interview requests before finally sharing his story at the end of his life. After Phar Lap, it took many years before Tommy formed another close bond. In 1977, his horse Reckless was the sentimental favourite to win the Melbourne Cup, but finished second.

Tommy was a gentleman whose tender care of a horse turned an unwanted animal into a national treasure. Today, Phar Lap remains a symbol of courage, a hero who achieved success when the odds were stacked against him. One is left to wonder how many more sporting mountains the big-hearted horse might have climbed.

Distinguished experts are often asked: who was the greatest racehorse in history? It is a mark of his enduring legacy that every great racehorse is compared to Phar Lap. The saying 'a heart as big as Phar Lap' alludes to true grit, gallantry and excellence in any worthwhile endeavour. Phar Lap stands tall as a benchmark for champions — magnificent in life, mysterious in death, immortal forever.

THE STORY OF HISTORY

Phar Lap's remarkable story has been commemorated by writers, filmmakers, sculptors and artists, and is celebrated in poetry and song. In his short life, an unwanted young horse became a legend who remains a drawcard in death, as he was in life. What we have left are his physical remains. Memorabilia, grainy photos and film footage preserve his magnificence so future generations can admire his greatness that lives on, undimmed by time.

It is safe to say we shall never see a horse like Phar Lap again. It was our nation's good fortune that the call to bolster flagging spirits was answered by a remarkable animal. Because of what he did, Australians and New Zealanders will always speak and write about Phar Lap. Many years after his death, the mystery of what happened to the Wonder Horse when he was at the peak of his powers continues to beat at our nation's heart.

In the search for the truth, there is much we do not know. Through this book, history hunters will be inspired to delve deeper into the mystery, to read more and, importantly, discover why a big red horse still means so much to young and old alike and why we still cheer him on.

PHAR LAP STATISTICS

Race record: 51 starts — 37 wins, 3 second placings and 2 third placings

Earnings: Calculated today, his race earnings would be the equivalent of over $15 million

Colour: Chestnut

Height: 17.1 hands (1.75 metres)

Bloodline: Night Raid (sire/father) and Entreaty (dam/mother)

Trainer/Strapper: Tommy Woodcock

Trainer/Owner: Harry Telford

Owner: David J. Davis

Principal jockeys: Jim Pike, Billy Elliot

MORE TO EXPLORE

Books

Armstrong, G. & Thompson, P. *Phar Lap: The Story of Australia's Greatest Ever Racehorse*. Stoke Hill Press, 2000.

Armstrong, G. & Thompson, P. *Phar Lap: How a Horse Became a Hero of His Time and an Icon of a Nation*. Allen & Unwin, 2003.

Barnard, J. *Phar Lap: A Brief History*. Museum of Victoria, 1991.

Benson, M. *Tommy Woodcock: The Story of Australia's Most Remarkable Trainer*. Shenley Publications, 1978.

Carter, I. *Phar Lap: The Story of the Big Horse*. Lansdowne Press, 1964.

Kirkwood, R. *The Phar Lap Collection*. BAS publishing, 2005.

Lowry, B. *Killing Phar Lap: An Untold Part of the Story*. AuthorHouse, 2014.

McEvoy, J. 'Phar Lap's Last Race' in *Great Horse Racing Mysteries*. Eclipse Press, 2000.

Putt, G. & McCord, P. *Phar Lap: The Untold Story*. BAS Publishing, 2009.

Reason, M. *Phar Lap: A True Legend*. Museum Victoria, 2009.

Wilkinson, M. *The Phar Lap Story*. Budget Books, 1983.

Wositzky, J. *Me & Phar Lap: The Remarkable Life of Tommy Woodcock*. Slattery Media Group, 2011.

Films

Phar Lap — a 1983 feature-length movie directed by Simon Wincer and written by David Williamson.

The Mighty Conqueror — a short documentary made in 1931; directed by Paulette McDonagh.

Podcast

Killing Phar Lap: A Forensic Investigation by Kerry Negara, 2020–2022.

Websites

collections.museumsvictoria.com.au/articles/3205

nma.gov.au/explore/collection/highlights/phar-lap-collection

nfsa.gov.au/collection/curated/phar-lap

nfsa.gov.au/latest/phar-lap-forever

SPECIAL THANKS

Alex Allan, Cate Sutherland, Naama Grey-Smith, Frank Greenwood, Lyne Greenwood, Frané Lessac, Kerry Negara, Barbara Lewis, Bruce and Helen Postle, Colleen Yarger (Curator of Library Collections, National Sporting Library & Museum, Virginia, USA), Marion E. Oster (Atherton Heritage Association), Graeme Putt, Dermot Henry (Head of Sciences, Museums Victoria Research Institute), Tanya Rajapakse (Project Officer, Sciences, Museums Victoria Research Institute), Alison Raaymakers (Senior Collection Manager, Australian Racing Museum) and reference librarians at the National Museum of New Zealand and the National Library of Australia.

Every effort has been made by the author to contact copyright holders and obtain permission to reproduce material in this book.

THE HISTORY HUNTER

Mark Greenwood is a History Hunter. He enjoys delving into slices of history, where themes like courage, hope and determination have played an essential role in defining our past.

To create *The Wonder Horse*, Mark visited the remains of Phar Lap's stables at Menlo Park, Atherton, California. He walked Phar Lap's old training track at Braeside Park and visited the exhibition at the Melbourne Museum where objects from Phar Lap's life, such as his training saddle, his horseshoes and Harry Telford's tonic book helped Mark tell the story of *The Wonder Horse*. For Mark, these journeys of discovery were crucial ingredients in bringing this History Hunter case file to life and helped him weave a story around one of the most enduring mysteries in Australian history.

Find out more at about Mark's award-winning books at markgreenwood.com.au.

JOIN THE HISTORY HUNTER FOR MORE . . .

THE DEADLY DIAMOND SAMPLE CHAPTER

No one knows the Hope Diamond's exact age other than to agree that it was conceived between one and three billion years ago. Its life began deep in the earth's mantle, one hundred and fifty kilometers below the planet's surface. Under intense heat and pressure, carbon atoms were compressed into the crystalised structure of a diamond — the hardest naturally occurring substance on earth.

After surviving birth in the firey throat of a volcano, and the violent eruption that brought it to the earth's surface in molten magma, the diamond came to rest on the Deccan Plateau in India. For millions of years, it remained entombed in solidified rock, tossed and tumbled in rivers of primeval slime that flowed from a ring of lofty mountains. Over time, the weathered rock casing eroded, freeing the diamond. In the sickle bend of the Krishna River, nature's miracle lay buried in the dirt.

Throughout the Middle Ages, extraordinary tales of a 'Valley of Diamonds' reached far beyond India to China, Arabia and Persia, before spreading to Europe. Books such as *One Thousand and One Nights*, *Sinbad the Sailor* and *The Travels of Marco Polo* described the strange lands where prized gems were found. Later texts described sacred temple idols with eyes fashioned from enormous diamonds.

The diamonds that came from the fabled mines of Golconda were highly valued. Local rulers jealously guarded the source and kept the largest diamonds for themselves. The radiance of these diamonds was legendary. Many believed they contained a supernatural force. Prized for colour, clarity, size and beauty, some were pure as a drop of dew. Others were orange or apricot, red or apple-green, canary-yellow or pale-rose-pink. But the rarest colour of all was midnight-blue.

An enormous blue diamond was said to have been worshipped as the all-seeing eye of a temple idol. One night a crowd gathered, drawn by the wailing of the Brahmin priests. A great sacrilege had occurred. A wicked thief had plucked the coveted gem from the eye of the sacred idol. A sorrowful chant was uttered, casting a curse forevermore on any mortal who possessed the idol's eye.

That legendary blue diamond and the curse placed on it continues to attract debate to this day. Does a haunting aura of bad luck really follow the diamond, casting a sinister spell from one owner to the next, causing illness, death and financial disaster?

TO FIND OUT MORE, READ THE DEADLY DIAMOND